Johann Sebastian

BACH

CONCERTO

for

THREE VIOLINS

and

ORCHESTRA

D MAJOR ♂ D-DUR

BWV1064

MUSIC MINUS ONE

SUGGESTIONS FOR USING THIS MMO EDITION

WE HAVE TRIED to create a product that will provide you an easy way to learn and perform this concerto with a full orchestra in the comfort of your own home. The following MMO features and techniques will help you maximize the effectiveness of the MMO practice and performance system:

Where the soloist begins a movement *solo*, we have provided an introductory measure with subtle taps inserted at the actual tempo before the soloist's entrance.

Chapter stops on your CD are conveniently located throughout the piece at the beginnings of practice sections, and are cross-referenced in the score. This should help you quickly find a desired place in the music as you learn the piece.

Because it involves a fixed orchestral performance, there is an inherent lack of flexibility in tempo.

We have observed generally accepted tempi, but some may wish to perform at a different tempo, or to slow down or speed up the accompaniment for practice purposes. In addition to the practice version included with this edition (see below), you can purchase from MMO specialized CD players & recorders which allow variable speed while maintaining proper pitch. This is an indispensable tool for the serious musician and you may wish to look into purchasing this useful piece of equipment for full enjoyment of all your MMO editions.

We want to provide you with the most useful practice and performance accompaniments possible. If you have any suggestions for improving the MMO system, please feel free to contact us. You can reach us by e-mail at *info@musicminusone.com*.

ABOUT THE 'PRACTICE TEMPO' VERSION

AS AN AID during the early stages of learning this concerto, we have included a second 'practice tempo' version of the faster outer movements of each accompaniment, which is identical to the main peformance, but has been slowed by approximately 20%. This will allow you to begin at a comfortably reduced speed until technique is more firmly in grasp, at which time the full-speed accompaniments can be substituted.

3193

CONTENTS

ISBN 978-1-59615-824-5

Concerto in D Major

for 3 Violins, Strings and Basso continuo
(BWV 1064)

Johann Sebastian Bach
1685-1750

Allegro

SOLO

99

101

103

105

108

112
cresc.

114
f   SOLO   *p*

116   TUTTI   SOLO

118

120
f

SOLO

Allegro

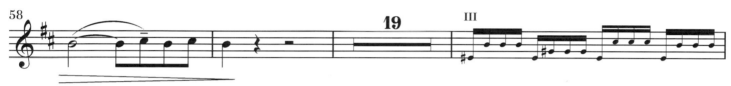

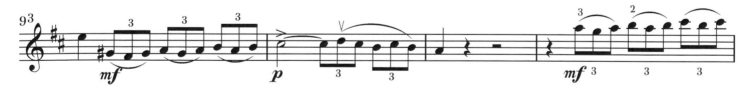

Concerto in D Major

for 3 Violins, Strings and Basso continuo
(BWV 1064)

Edited by Mario Hossen

Johann Sebastian Bach
1685-1750

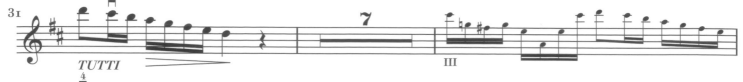

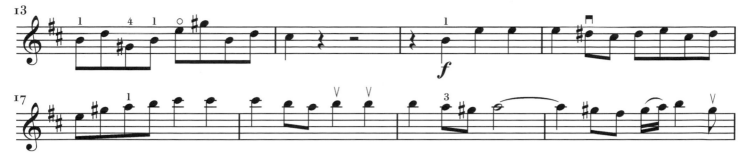

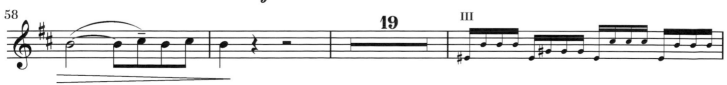

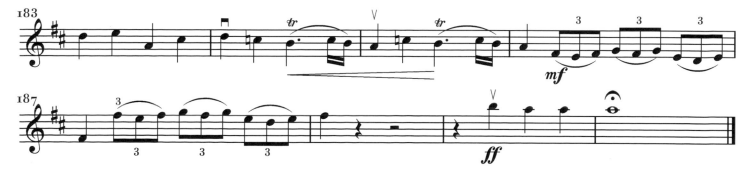

Violin Solo III

Edited by Mario Hossen

Concerto in D Major

for 3 Violins, Strings and Basso continuo
(BWV 1064)

Johann Sebastian Bach
(1685-1750)

Allegro

MMO 3193

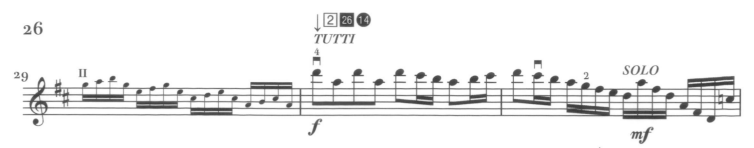

Adagio

Allegro

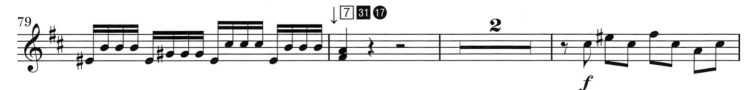

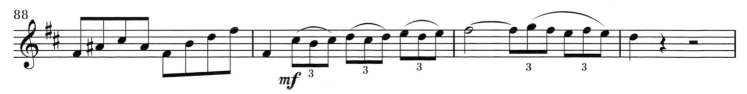

MUSIC MINUS ONE
50 Executive Boulevard - Elmsford, NY 10523
1.800.449.6474 (USA) - 914.592.1188 Int'l
www.musicminusone.com

MMO 3193   Pub. No. 0959   Printed in USA